D0561369

Stuff Every

HUSBAND

Should Know

Library of Congress Cataloging in Publication Number: 2010936314

ISBN: 978-1-59474-497-6

Printed in Malaysia

Typeset in Goudy and Monotype Old Style

Design by Jenny Kraemer
Illustrations by Kate Francis
Production management by John J. McGurk

Quirk Books
215 Church Street
Philadelphia, PA 19106
www.quirkbooks.com

10 9 8 7 6 5 4 3 2 1

Stuff Every Lawyer Should Know: The publisher and author hereby disclaim any liability from an injury that may result from the use, proper or improper, of the information contained in this book. We do not guarantee that this information is safe, complete, or wholly accurate, nor should it be considered a substitute for a reader's good judgment and common sense. In other words: Exercise caution when walking your wife home from the theater. Be safe when serving hot food in bed. And no matter what she says, never ever agree that yes, that dress does indeed make her look fat.

Stuff Every

HUSBAND

Should Know

By Eric San Juan

QUIRK BOOKS
PHILADELPHIA

To my wife,
for not laughing *too* hard when you found out
I was writing this book.

Introduction

No one ever tells you what marriage is really like.

From married men it's a wry, knowing laugh: "You don't know *what* you're getting into, kid." From married women it's a laundry list of what their husbands do wrong, capped with the unhelpfully vague command to treat *your* wife well.

But worst of all is the marital advice that amounts to either "Your wife is always right" or "You need to put her in her place." Both are wrong.

Marriage is about forming a single unit out of two people. Accomplishing this is (a) awesome and (b) a lot of work. Your role as a husband is to put the happiness of the marriage before your personal desires; your role as a man is to be a man. Despite rumors to the contrary, these two things are not mutually exclusive.

This book is about striking that balance. It's about manning up and being a good husband, because being a good husband makes for a happy wife, and a happy wife makes for a happy you. It's about retaining your manhood and using your manhood in service of your wife's happiness.

Think of this book as a sympathetic, helpful older brother: been there, did something stupid, suffered the consequences, came through okay on the other side. Someone who wants to spare you the heartache of going through all the stupid bits yourself. Whether we're talking about fixing a hole in the wall or coping with joint shopping trips, there are ways to make your life together more pleasant every day. And throughout a marriage, you're gonna have a lot of days.

Naturally, your wife is a unique individual, and not every single piece of advice in this book is 100 percent applicable to every marriage. Nonetheless, we think you'll find that most of this stuff is universal. All husbands and wives are different . . . and yet the issues they face are often strikingly familiar.

So sit back, flip through the pages, and get ready for married life. It won't be easy, but you're a man. You'll deal with it.

Regarding the

WIFE

The Ten Commandments of Marriage

A happy, healthy marriage begins and ends with the basics.

1. The kids come first. If there are no kids, your wife comes first.

2. Be kind. A cruel word, once said, cannot be unsaid.

3. Your wife is always the most beautiful woman you've ever seen.

4. Your wife is always the best sex you've ever had.

5. Everything is your fault. Learn to embrace this.

6. When your wife says "fine," it means she is not happy.

7. Don't seek to change each other; seek to accept each other.

8. Let the past stay in the past. Your marriage is about today and tomorrow.

9. Your wedding anniversary and your wife's birthday are the most important holidays of the year.

10. Laugh. A lot. Laugh *with* her. Laugh *at* yourself.

Words to Forget You Ever Knew

Let's take care of this up front. "Honesty is always the best policy"—well, yes, *generally speaking*, but taking that wisdom to unnecessary extremes has destroyed more marriages than strip clubs and World of Warcraft combined. If you want a long and loving relationship, you're going to have to accept that some things you just cannot say out loud. So *think* the following all you like—though even there we recommend treading with caution—as long as you remember: Don't. Ever. Say them.

- "Shut up."
- "How could you be so stupid?"
- "Have you put on weight?"
- "What did you do to your hair?"
- (In reference to someone other than your wife, unless your wife is a bisexually inclined horndog) "She's got fantastic [body part]."
- "This is your fault."

- (During a disagreement) "My mother was right."
- "How hard could it have been to make this? Anyone can follow a recipe."
- (If she is a housewife) "Well, *someone* has to go to work around here."

Stuff You Should Learn How to Say

Just as there are some negative things you must never say to your wife, there are plenty of positive things you *should* say, and often. Write them down on your hand so you don't forget. Practice in a mirror, if you must. Just understand that happy marriages are built on generous use of the following, presented as the situation warrants.

- "You look beautiful."
- "I was wrong."
- "I love you."
- "You're right."
- "Dinner was delicious."
- "I shouldn't have done that. I'm sorry."
- "Would you like a back rub?"

How to Make Decisions

What to have for dinner? What color to paint the bedroom? What to how the when why you where the who? Marriage can be an endless series of decisions, and after a long day at work making decision after decision, *yet another one* can feel like a backbreaker. Making day-to-day marital decisions, however, is easier than it seems.

- **Don't over-think.** Thinking is good. We encourage it. But you can go too far. If you're hemming and hawing, it's time to say A or B.

- **If it "doesn't matter," it doesn't matter.** Don't care if you have beef or chicken for dinner? Don't *say* you don't care, just pick one and stick with it.

- **Be willing to research.** For tough decisions, don't rely on manly know-how. In the Internet age, research is easy. Know your facts, *then* decide.

- **Second-guessing is not allowed.** Train yourself on this. When you make a decision, it's made. Unless you . . .

- **Get more information.** Never be anything but open to new information. A good husband can adapt.

- **It's not life and death.** You will be asked to make many decisions. They will often be inconsequential. Afraid you'll get it wrong? Pffft. You're a man. You'll live with the results.

How to Drive Together in Peace

Ninety-nine percent of married people hate the way their spouse drives. That's not a scientific poll, but the anecdotal evidence is pretty convincing. Fortunately, there are ways to chill out about it.

- **Leave on time.** Few things increase stress more than being late, and stress makes for snippy spouses.

- **Don't be a driving instructor.** As much as you want to show her the "correct" way to drive, don't. Adults don't want to be taught as if they're children—especially by the man they love.

- **Save the rage.** If you want to shout at other drivers when you're alone in the car, have at it. Do so when driving with your wife, however, and you'll end up fighting with her rather than the other driver.

- **You're not Jeff Gordon.** Driving like a madman makes passengers nervous. And nervous passengers won't want to sleep with you later.

- **Turn driving time into quality time.** *Talk.* Don't talk about household troubles—talk about your lottery fantasies, favorite movies from childhood, and the fun you'd like to have the next time you two are alone.

- **Radio is your friend.** Listening to a program you both enjoy—talk radio, audio books, podcasts—not only distracts you both from roadway irritants, it gives you something to bond over.

- **Play driving games.** The Alphabet Game, spotting license plates, and other distractions aren't just for kids. Use car time to add fun to your marriage.

- **She controls the climate.** You're a man. You'll deal with it.

Learn to Listen
(or at Least Pretend To)

The old wisdom that communication is one of the keys to a good marriage is true enough. What those who dispense such wisdom sometimes forget to mention is that inbound communication is more important than outbound. The guy cliché that women are *incomprehensible!* is wrong and comes from laziness. Any husband who practices listening to his wife will eventually find that he can indeed follow her thoughts, even if he would never think them himself.

1. **Listening is not the art of silence.** It is the art of considering. A good listener doesn't just shut up and let his spouse speak—he hears her words, processes them, and tries to understand what sparked them in the first place.

2. **Maintain eye contact with your wife.** Looking away while she speaks not only invites distraction, it sends the message that what she's saying is not important to

you. And what your wife says to you is always important—even when it's not.

3. **Imagine that her point of view is yours.** Yes, even if her point of view includes purchasing a smaller television. The simple act of pretending to be her for a few moments will not only help you navigate the minefield of spousal communication, it will help you better understand your wife and make you seem like a thoughtful husband.

4. **You don't need to have the last word.** Sure, you want to—we all like to declare things definitively—but now that you're a husband, the more important thing to remember is that you *don't* want your wife to feel that you think your thoughts are more important than hers. Letting her have the last word shows that you respect her as an equal.

Six Great, Easy Dates

The courtship might be over, but the days of having a great time together are only just beginning. Married dates don't have to be elaborate and expensive affairs made to impress. It's easy to keep things fresh without spending a lot of time and money. Here are six suggestions for easy dates that still manage to pack in fun, romance, and good times.

1. **Movie night.** Dinner and a movie is always a classic date, but why not take it a step further and designate a weekly movie night? You can even stay home instead of going out. What's important is that regular dose of Couple Time.

2. **Bike ride.** If the sun is out and the weather is warm, hop on bikes and go for a ride. In the local park, around the neighborhood, to the bookstore—where doesn't matter. What matters is your time together.

3. **Local theater.** You probably have a local community playhouse and don't even

realize it. Area schools put on productions, too. Go take in a show. It's not Broadway, but it doesn't need to be.

4. **Living-room-floor sleepover party.** Push the furniture aside, spread the couch cushions on the floor, turn off the TV, turn on the radio, open a bottle of wine, and camp out on the living-room floor. Simple as it is, upending your comfort zone will be tremendous fun.

✦ *Living-room-floor sleepover party* ✦

5. **Fruit picking.** You're probably closer than you realize to a "you-pick" farm. The premise is simple: You grab a basket and walk around the fields picking your own apples, strawberries, whatever's in season. Not only is it a great afternoon in the sun, you'll reap the rewards later when you prepare meals with hand-picked goodies.

6. **Swap meet/flea market.** It's not about the shopping, it's about walking around together looking at an eclectic array of junk. Strolling through rows of oddball items and even odder people won't cost you a dime, and you'll have something to talk about afterward.

Five Great, Classy Dates

OK, so we suggested a few easy dates designed to keep the fun in your marriage, but that doesn't mean you should do *only* easy dates. Your wife deserves a touch of class every now and then, too, you cheapskate.

1. **Upscale restaurant.** Let her break out that cute black dress, wear the expensive shoes she's only worn once, and spend an hour on her hair. When your wife feels like a woman, the rewards extend well beyond the great dinner and atmosphere.

2. **Theater/opera/philharmonic/ballet.** No skimping on local and amateur groups this time. Spend the time and money, dress nice, and take her to the big city for a dose of the arts. She'll love it, and one night won't kill you. Your beer and pretzels aren't going anywhere.

3. **Museum.** If you're within two hours of an urban area, you're probably within two hours of a good museum. Spend an

afternoon looking at art you don't understand and can't afford and then have a late lunch in an elegant café. Don't worry. That uncomfortable "cultured" feeling goes away after a few hours.

4. **Wine tasting.** "Classy" doesn't have to be expensive. Local wineries and other elegant establishments often offer wine tastings. They won't cost you much, and they are a good excuse to dress nicely, act refined, and eat smelly cheese.

5. **Ballroom dancing lessons.** That's right, tough guy. Suck it up and take a few with your wife. She'll feel like a lady, you'll look like a superhero no matter how klutzy you are, and all that time spent pressed close together is likely to have other benefits.

How to Serve Breakfast in Bed

In the grand game of scoring husband points, few moves are bigger winners than serving your lovely lady breakfast in bed. It takes a little work, especially if you're inept in the kitchen, but the rewards are more than worth the effort.

1. Be sure to have the necessary ingredients on hand, including a tray—one with fold-down legs so that it can be used in someone's lap. This may require some shopping the day before.

2. A surprise is always better, so wake up early. First thing: Put on the coffee or tea.

3. Time to cook. Prepare *quietly* if you intend it to be a surprise. What you make depends on your expertise. A simple breakfast of toast, cereal, fresh fruit and a hard-boiled egg is easiest, but even someone who can't cook can handle toaster waffles, precooked bacon, and slices of melon. If you've got the skills, go full bore and prepare eggs to her liking, with bacon or sausage, toast,

and fresh fruit. Don't worry if you're a bad cook. What counts is the gesture.

4. Arrange the finished food on the tray, alongside a cup of juice and a cup of coffee or tea prepared to her liking. If you want to really go nuts, place a small vase and flower on the tray, too.

5. Adorn the presentation with a small handwritten note professing your love.

6. Wake your darling—*before* you put the tray on the bed; spilled messes are *not* awesome—and prepare to bask in her sweet, sweet love.

7. Finally, clean up the kitchen while she eats. No one wants to crawl out of bed to a mess.

How to Choose Great Jewelry

Few things vex a man more than picking out jewelry. Choose wrong and it's an expensive failure. Choose well, however, and score huge husband points.

- **Go simple.** The showier the piece, the more likely it will clash with her taste. Elegance never goes out of style.

- **Follow her lead.** If she already owns platinum earrings adorned with diamonds, choose a platinum necklace or bracelet with diamonds.

- **Know how she dresses.** If she wears low-cut blouses, choose a pendant to accent her . . . look. If she wears her hair up or short, earrings are a great choice.

- **Use a regular jeweler.** If you made a home-run purchase in the past, return to the same jeweler. Explain what you bought last time and ask for recommendations on a matching piece.

- **Think long-term.** If you think she'll like those black pearl earrings, ask the jeweler about a matching set. Purchase items from the set over the next several birthdays or holidays.

- **Flatter her face.** The shape of her earrings should be *different* from that of her face. Angular earrings look great on round-faced women, round earrings are perfect for women with narrow or angular faces, short earrings complement long faces, etc.

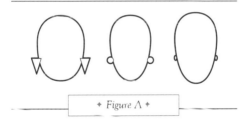

+ *Figure A* +

- **Flatter her body.** Long necklaces make her look taller; chokers emphasize her petite nature. Tiny bracelets for tiny women. Wide ring bands for women with long fingers.

- **Know your colors.** Tell the jeweler her hair and eye color to help you find a piece to complement her look.

Meeting Her Friend's Husband

Your wife's friend's husband. You simply *have* to meet him! She just *knows* you two will get along! The matchmaking wife is an inevitable part of marriage. You will be put in a position where your wife expects (read: hopes) you'll hit it off with her good friend's husband. You can make it work more often than you realize.

- **Talk.** The stereotypical guy doesn't talk about what makes him tick, but the best way to test the waters is to be open about what interests you. Love the Cowboys? Say so. An avid video gamer? Say that, too. You'll turn him away or make a new friend. Either is fine.

- **Be open-minded.** Most of these "matches" will fail miserably, but you should still give the guy a chance. You just might find a good buddy you didn't know existed.

- **Alcohol.** This social issue often pops up early. Allow him to open the door. If you drink, follow his lead; if you don't, say so.

- **Be honest.** If you *really* dislike the guy, tell your wife. She can continue spending time with her friend solo rather than trying to force you into it.

- **Could be a new friend? Embrace it.** If you only think of him as "your wife's friend's husband," you may be losing out. And as we get older, good friends are harder to find.

- **Don't forsake your longtime friends.** Not only will you look like a jerk, you'll grow to resent your wife for it. If you're hanging as a couple with *her* friends, then it's only fair you also hang as a couple with *yours*.

The Quick Weekend Getaway: Why and How

"Every day till death do you part" adds up to a *lot* of dirty dishes and laundry. Yeah, getting all the chores done is important—but when one or both of you have been drowning in work for months, and your next vacation is far off over the horizon, it may be time to take your wife by the hand, boldly declare, "You're a princess, not a maid!" and spend the weekend abandoning domesticity in favor of a whirlwind romance. A spontaneous getaway needn't be complicated to put a smile on her face and yours: With minimal effort, you can be the kind of hero who sets his wife's heart (and libido) aflutter.

- **Don't waste time traveling.** You want your interlude to start *now*, and a mere 30 minutes from home is plenty of distance to leave behind the daily grind. Google "weekend" and your geographical area; destinations will present themselves.

- **Save your money, too.** You don't need to pay a lot for the privilege of enjoying your wife's company. Try exploring a national park: Sightseeing is a simple pleasure, one of the cheapest romantic activities there is.

- **Think seclusion.** A cabin by a lake, a bungalow with a big tub, a room in a bed-and-breakfast. When the two of you are alone together with no agenda, no clock ticking, nothing that *needs* to be done, it ought to seem perfectly natural to . . . do that other thing. For as long as you want.

- **Spend two nights if you can.** But even a one-night weekend of pure escapism is a hundred times more exciting than the same old same old.

- **Nature's not her cup of tea?** Find a charming little neighborhood somewhere whose Main Street has cafés and shops. Buy her two things unbidden: a small sugary treat and a sentimental souvenir. The former will get you a kiss now; the latter will get you many in the months to come.

That Time of the Month and You

On the best of days your wife is a riddle, wrapped in a mystery, tucked inside an enigma—that's why you love her, after all—but few days leave you as flummoxed as those that fall during That Time of the Month. You know what time we mean. And you want to know how to get through it.

- **Put it on your own calendar.** It's not as bad when it doesn't catch you by surprise.

- **Don't point out that it's That Time of the Month.** She knows. Drawing attention to it or suggesting that she's acting unusual will probably only irritate her.

- **Control your libido.** If she's interested, let her come to you. Otherwise, let her deal with her feminine burden without your wandering hands.

- **Avoid difficult family decisions.** Mood swings during the menstrual cycle aren't a sexist stereotype, they're a medical fact. Make life easier by putting off tough choices when possible.

- **Don't blame disagreements on PMS.** Just don't do it. It's unfair to your wife and it makes you look like a thoughtless jerk.

- **Provide back rubs and neck massages.** (Unless your wife is feeling uncomfortable and disinclined to be touched, in which case never mind.)

- **Cook her favorite meal.** A little comfort food goes a long way. And hey, you get to eat, too. Bonus.

- **Never suggest her period is inconvenient for you.** If *you* don't like it, how do you think *she* feels?

How to Dress Yourself

Some men are born with an innate sense of what clothing looks good in every situation. And then there's the rest of us. Thankfully, a few years of marriage can teach a thing or two about dressing ourselves:

- **Say "no" to the T.** T-shirts are great. Some might say they're *the greatest*. But, as an adult, you're obliged to skip them when going out to dinner, on dates with your wife, or when attending your child's graduation. Sorry.

- **Clean out the closet.** If you wore it regularly while in college, it's a safe bet that you should toss it. You get to keep that one old shirt you really love, but that's it.

- **Ask for her input.** If your wife thinks it looks awful on you, trust her. Always.

- **Own an all-purpose suit.** Don't go for trendy or modern. Unless you need it for business, you might wear it only once every few years, so get something simple and timeless.

✦ *How to Dress Yourself* ✦

- **Get dress shoes.** You might think a pair of boots and some sneakers are all you need. You're wrong. You need dress shoes. Pick something simple and in a "matches everything" color like black.

- **Your shoes and belt should match.** That's just how it works.

- **Don't forget to groom.** If you could see the author, you'd see a scruffy mess . . . unless it's for an important function. Then the razor comes out. Even if you're usually a mess, learn to clean up well.

Women's Clothing Sizes: WTF?

Calculus. Quantum mechanics. The last half hour of *2001: A Space Odyssey*. All of these are easier to grasp than women's sizes.

- **Bras:** The number equals the number of inches a woman measures beneath her breasts. The letter, or cup size, represents the fullness of her breast. *Complexity Level*: Complicated but logical. The number is determined by measuring just below the breast, adding five if it's an odd number and four if it's even. Then measure around the fullest part of the breast. The difference between the two numbers determines the cup size: A 1-inch difference is an A cup, 2 inches is a B cup, 3 inches is a C cup, etc.

- **Shoes:** A woman's shoe size in America is always 1½ more than the same size men's shoe. If your wife wears a 10, that's like a men's 8½. *Complexity Level*: Feet are easier to understand than breasts . . . but a whole lot less interesting.

- **Everything else:** If we took this whole book to break down what women's sizes mean, it still wouldn't make any sense. They vary from brand to brand and from year to year. There is no way to estimate or understand your wife's shirt, pant, or dress size, and if you guess either high or low she will be lastingly unhappy about it. Just sneak a peek at the tags on things she wears frequently and proceed accordingly. *Complexity Level:* We can land a man on the moon, but Albert Einstein and Stephen Hawking working together for a decade would be unable to figure out this insanity.

Looking at Other Women Politely

You are man, not machine, genetically wired to notice that ladies are lovely creatures. Getting married doesn't change that. Touching is off-limits, obviously, but looking is your biological imperative. Just don't be a sleaze about it, OK?

- **Your head is not a swivel.** Your wife doesn't need to see your head-turning antics. It's tacky and disrespectful. Take whatever glimpse you can get and be happy with that. Meanwhile, keep one eye on the wife and know where *she's* looking. It's like hunting; You've got to be aware of your surroundings at all times if you want to bag any prey.

- **No commentary, please.** Even if your wife is okay with you looking, keep the "Oh wow!" commentary to yourself. Again, tacky and disrespectful.

- **Don't let it linger.** Yes, your impulse is to stare, because *wow*, did you *see* her? But don't. Learn to slam your glances the same way you do shots: fast.

- **She gets to look, too.** This should be a given, yet far too many guys think *they* get a pass but their wife isn't allowed to ogle other dudes. Sorry, fellas, it doesn't work that way. If you get to look, so does she.

How to Remember Things Men Don't Remember

A deer in headlights ain't got nothin' on a husband caught forgetting his anniversary. And let's face it, we husbands are good at forgetting things that don't involve red meat, fuel-injected engines, hi-def screens, or spherical objects being thrown, kicked, or hit. Remembering not to forget and forgetting to remember are easy, but remembering to remember is . . . wait, what?

- **Your anniversary:** Inscribe the date inside your wedding band. Tell your wife it's because you want to remember that day forever. You'll look romantic. You're really just being smart.

- **Her birthday:** Register with a Web site like Memotome.com or Forlater.net to automatically e-mail reminders directly to your inbox. Also, Web sites like Ftd.com let you schedule a flower or gift delivery months ahead. Put down this book and go place an order. Seriously, do it. Right now. That way, even if you forget, she'll never know.

- **Upcoming events:** Write them down. The very act of jotting down the date will help embed it in your memory. Consider putting them all on a calendar that hangs at eye level near where you keep your keys, so you see it every day. (*Not* on your fridge! When dudes go to the fridge, our eyes don't even start functioning until the door is open and we can see the food.)

- **Her friend's name:** Associate it with a brief, distinctive visual characteristic. Alliteration can help make it even more memorable. "Cathy, curly hair. Gloria, gangly arms."

- **Her favorite flower/perfume/etc.:** Again, think visually. Link the flower with a characteristic you associate with your wife. Tulips = her tasty lips. Yellow roses = her hot yellow dress. And so on.

- **When to buy new household supplies:** Let's not beat around the bush: We're talking about toilet paper, and you should buy some every time you're in a store that sells it. Now that you're married, *there is no such thing as too much toilet paper*.

How to Survive Shopping Together

"Oh, dear God, she's asking me to go shopping. I skipped out on that last thing, so now I *have* to suck it up and do this. But she's going to try on clothes *all day*! The horror. *The horror*."

- **Liking everything will backfire.** Think telling her that you like every skirt she tries on will speed things up? Think again. It will only make her decision tougher. Have a real opinion. Hate a few things, pick one, and say it looks *great*. That will get you both out the door faster.

- **Schedule something for later.** Plan a time-sensitive activity—dinner reservations, a party, etc.—later in the day to add deadline pressure to the shopping experience.

- **Turn it into a date.** Enhance the shopping expedition with date stuff: lunch at a romantic cafe, a glass of wine at the elegant winery, a walk on the beach, and the promise of post-shopping fooling around.

- **Plan your own shopping around it.** Hey, you need stuff, too, right? Use the time to take care of Numero Uno.

- **Bring another couple.** She's got someone to shop with, you've got someone to commiserate with. Go out for dinner and drinks afterward. A winning situation for one and all.

Be the Master of One Meal a Day

You may not be the world's greatest chef, but even you can keep Gordon Ramsay from having a seizure by keeping a few basics in mind. More important, unless your wife is that rare creature who loves the kitchen more than anywhere else in the world, it's only fair to realize that, if she's burdened with being crowned queen of dinner, you can at least be king of breakfast—or vice versa. So, here are the basics.

Breakfast

Eggs are your friend. Eggs are the all-purpose tool of breakfast. Get friendly with them and you'll have an endless array of options available. Start with plain old scrambled eggs; it's an easy, quick fry that, as you get the hang of it, can pick up an onion here, some cheese there, until before you know it you're inventing your own omelets.

Meat your breakfast. Cooking breakfast meats (or their fake-meat vegetarian counterparts) is so easy even an amateur can do it. Just fry in a pan until they look done. No training required.

Lunch

A dish best served cold. Because great lunches are often cold, you can master this one minus any cooking skills whatsoever. Remember: sharp cheese complements tangy meat; cold pasta salads are a cinch; roasted red peppers, sun-dried tomatoes, and the like turn ordinary deli sandwiches into gourmet delights.

Leftovers are your friend. Leftovers don't need to be a repeat of last night. Learn to mix and match from various (*recent*) batches to create new meals. Simple, easy, effective.

Dinner

Master the pasta. There is no more versatile food than pasta. Know how to make a variety of simple sauces and gravies (see "How to Make a Great Marinara Sauce") and you'll have dozens of easy meals at your disposal.

Grilling greatness. Weekend grillers dish out red steaks and dry burgers. You can do better than that. Marinate steaks to make them tender. Add mango, peach, or citrus to store-bought BBQ sauce to make it shine.

How to Make a Great Marinara Sauce

Want to pitch in on cooking duties without having to navigate the complex intricacies of the kitchen? You'll have dozens of meals at your fingertips simply by knowing how to make a great marinara sauce. Here are two easy varieties that will have you turning up your nose at the jarred stuff.

Classic Marinara

Ingredients: 1 to 2 tablespoons olive oil; 1 small onion, diced; 1 carrot, diced; 1 celery stalk, diced; 2 garlic cloves, peeled and crushed; pinch crushed red pepper flakes; salt (optional); 1 bay leaf; 1 28-ounce can crushed tomatoes; bunch fresh basil, roughly chopped

1. Put olive oil in a pan over medium heat. Add onion, carrot, celery, garlic, pepper, salt (if using), and bay leaf and sauté until vegetables are tender and it smells real good.

2. Add crushed tomatoes. Lower heat and simmer 20–25 minutes.

3. Remove and discard bay leaf. Remove pan from heat.

4. Puree sauce using an immersion blender, food processor, or blender until smooth.

5. Stir in basil.

Tomato Herb Cream Sauce

Ingredients: 1 tablespoon olive oil; 2 garlic cloves, peeled and crushed; crushed red pepper flakes to taste; 1 28-ounce can crushed tomatoes; ½ cup heavy cream; bunch fresh basil, roughly chopped; few sprigs fresh parsley, roughly chopped; ¼ to ½ cup grated Parmesan cheese

1. Again: Olive oil goes in the pan over medium heat. Add garlic, pepper, tomato, and cream and sauté for about ten minutes, until garlic is fragrant and onions are translucent.

2. Stir basil and parsley into sauce.

3. Add cheese and stir until mixed thoroughly. Simmer another few minutes.

What to Do with Them

- Switch pastas. Meat tortellini one night, angel hair the next, cheese ravioli another, next time some shells, and so on.

- Add more cheese for a creamier taste. Add a quarter cup of vodka to the herb cream sauce to turn it into vodka sauce. The possibilities are endless.

- Bake with layered meat, cheese, and either ziti or lasagna.

How to Grocery Shop in Less Than 30 Minutes

Before you can cook anything, you need food. The trick is getting the food without getting trapped in endless supermarket hell.

- **Lists, lists, lists.** Even if you never actually use a list, the act of making one will help you keep the essentials in mind. A focused hunt is a successful hunt.

- **Skip the cart.** If you can get away with using a hand basket, do. Shopping-cart traffic jams are worse than Manhattan gridlock.

- **Hit the butcher first.** Place your meat order, go shop, and then come back to pick it up. Time spent waiting is time wasted.

- **Buy only what you need.** The aisles are no place for improv. Know in advance what meals you'll be making and what they require, and buy just that.

- **Learn to bag.** You can shave precious minutes off the checkout experience if you're a good bagger. Beverages and cans go in first; bread goes in last.

Regarding the

HOME

Stuff You Should Know Before You Buy a House

Deciding to get married and then becoming parents are the only two choices you'll make that are bigger than the decision to buy a house. You're not just choosing a place to rest your head at night, you're choosing a place to build a life. The place where your children will take their first steps. The place that will play host to your massive television. Before taking the plunge, here's what you need to know.

- Build or buy? You'll pay about 20 percent more for a new home, but you'll also have more control over floor plan, amenities, and the like.

- Get a loan preapproval before you choose a home. Knowing how much you can afford will streamline an already difficult process.

- Hire a purchasing agent. They will know an overpriced property when they see it, spot new listings before they go public, and help navigate negotiations. Spend a little now, save a lot later.

- The average stay in a new home is six to ten years, so keep that in mind.

- Home inspections are your friend. Even if the house looks immaculate and well maintained, have it inspected before you buy.

- You're not looking for your dream home, you're looking for your *wife's* dream home. Let's face it: Your domestic needs are pretty simple. So find a place that (a) makes her happy and (b) you're OK with.

- Know the neighborhood. That house might be a steal because it's down the street from a waste-disposal facility or creepy old burial ground.

- Ask about casements, wildlife areas, and zoning restrictions. You'll want to know you can't build that pool before you buy, not after.

- That nearby empty lot or patch of woods won't be undeveloped forever. Research local zoning before you buy; you don't want to be staring at an oil refinery in a few years.

- Skip the electric oven. Gas ranges last longer (15 years on average).

- When it comes to remodeling, bathrooms are your top priority. They have the highest return on investment—more than 100 percent! (Kitchens are second.)

- If the floor is not level, steer clear. Costly repairs are in this house's future.

- Even if you don't have kids, buy in a town that has a good school system. Doing so will help your home retain value.

The Give-and-Take of Choosing a Home

Whether you're renting or buying, choosing a home requires a mountain of compromise. More often than not, you will (or should) defer to your wife's desires. Sometimes, though, you need to stand your ground. The key to compromising on this big issue is to pick your battles.

- **Bathroom must satisfy both.** Bathroom-related issues are a major cause of tension between spouses. More than any other room, you'll work to share this one amicably— so when you're scoping out potential homes, if either of you is unhappy with it, think twice. Also, listen closely to your wife's concerns; she'll be in there more than you. Note: If you can afford a place with two bathrooms, DO IT.

- **Kitchen vs. leisure space.** If need be, be prepared to bend here. A lot of life goes on in the kitchen, which means a great finished kitchen is a higher priority than a giant rec room.

- **Massive TV vs. living-room comfort.** As much as you want the greatest television known to man, the primary criterion for choosing a living room is not whether there's enough wall space for a plasma. You want general comfort, good lighting, access to the rest of the house, and a nice view. Seek balance.

- **Choose one feature, and stand your ground.** You get one feature to stand firm on, so choose it well. Spacious backyard? Full garage? Finished basement? Choose one and insist on it.

- **Choose one feature, and give in.** See how we said to choose one feature and stick to your guns? Your wife gets to do the same. Know what is most important to her. Master bedroom? Kitchen? Wrap-around porch? Be sure she gets it. It makes getting your own chosen feature that much easier.

- **Neighborhood vs. commute.** "Location, location, location" doesn't just mean your neighborhood, it means proximity to your workplace. If you accept a lengthy commute, you accept the idea of never enjoying your own home. And that, dear reader, stinks. Be sure to balance the two.

Painting a Room Is Easy

See the title at the top of this page? It says "Painting a Room Is Easy" because painting a room is easy.

1. Remove furniture, rugs, etc., from the room. Cover what you can't move with a tarp, old blankets, or plastic sheets.

2. Remove outlets, switch plates, etc., or simply cover with masking or painter's tape.

3. Fix flaws in the walls (see "How to Do Simple Wall Repairs," page 68). Remove nails and other protrusions. Sand walls using a pole sander.

4. Thoroughly clean all surfaces to be painted. Dust or residue will leave bumps in the paint.

5. With masking or painter's tape, frame out areas that won't be painted (windows, molding, door frames, etc.)

6. Lay down a drop cloth. Ensure entire floor is covered.

7. If necessary, apply primer to walls. You'll need to prime if painting plain drywall or unpainted wood. No need if you're going over existing paint.

8. With a brush, paint a two-inch band at all corners, along molding, and where the walls meet the floor/ceiling.

9. Paint. Use a roller. Make sure the roller is covered completely in paint, but not dripping wet. Use vertical strokes.

10. Let dry (not longer than 24 hours), then remove the tape. Using a small brush, touch up imperfections.

11. Let room dry completely. Replace hardware and furniture.

How to Do Simple Wall Repairs

It doesn't matter if you poked unnecessary holes while installing your new plasma, clipped the wall while rearranging the furniture for your wife, or had an elaborate bathroom accident involving shaving cream, a toothbrush, and handstands. Something happened, your wall is no longer pristine, and it's time to rectify that problem.

Fixing Small Holes

1. Place premixed joint compound (available at home-improvement stores) into a pan or container.

2. Use a spackle knife to spread compound across the damaged area. Apply two coats, the second more extensive than the first. (Note: With some compounds, you may have to lightly dampen the wall first. Check the package.)

3. Let dry, sand lightly, and repaint.

Fixing Large Holes

1. Cut a rectangular patch of new drywall large enough to cover the hole.

2. Place new drywall over the damaged area and trace the outline onto the wall (*Figure A*).

3. Using a drywall saw or utility knife, cut out the damaged drywall along your tracing lines (*Figure B*). Be sure to check inside the wall before cutting to ensure there are no wires. If you need to break away more wall to look, do so; you're going to repair it anyway.

4. There are several methods for mounting a drywall patch. The most common are either to affix drywall clips to the wall opening, near the corners, or to cut strips of plywood or drywall to act as a backing board. Strips should be several inches taller than the hole and will be placed inside the hole, behind the wall.

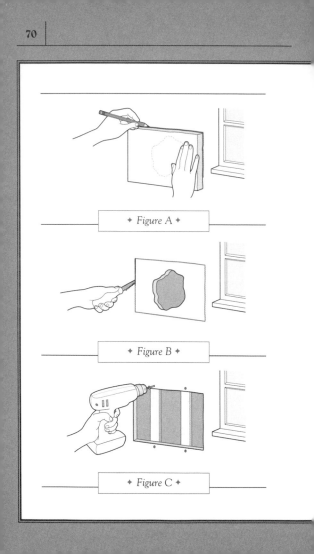

+ Figure A +

+ Figure B +

+ Figure C +

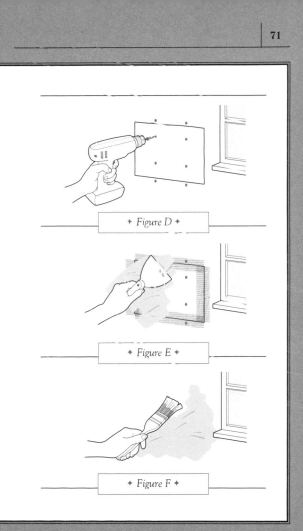

✦ Figure D ✦

✦ Figure E ✦

✦ Figure F ✦

5. Use drywall screws to attach the clips or backing strips to the wall (*Figure C*).

6. Place the drywall patch snugly into the hole. Affix to the clips or backing strips using drywall screws (*Figure D*).

7. Apply adhesive drywall tape to the edges of the patch job.

8. Apply compound as described in "Fixing Small Holes" (*Figure E*). Sand lightly until smooth; repaint (*Figure F*).

Wife Space Comes Before Man Cave

Few things can get a man as starry-eyed as day-dreaming about his man cave: a nice television, maybe a pool table, and a mini-fridge stocked with some cold ones. And hey, wouldn't a humidor go nicely in the corner by the big-screen video-game setup? But, as a married man, you have priorities— and your man cave is not at the top of the list. Your wife's space (read: the rest of the house) must be in order before you get your playroom; otherwise you send her the message that you're still a bachelor at heart. Some specific tips:

- No matter who is the primary cook, the kitchen always comes first. It's at the dinner table that houses are turned into homes.

- If an item looks like it would be at home in a frat house or teenager's room, it doesn't belong in the living room and will be a constant annoyance to your wife.

- Generally speaking, men do not have the kind of close relationship with the bathroom that women have. Therefore, you should get out of the way and let your wife arrange the bathroom as she sees fit. You pee on trees. You'll adapt.

- Man caves are, by definition, male retreats. If your relationship is on the rocks, a man cave will only make it worse.

How to Keep House (Without Forsaking Guy Time)

As much as your daydreams may say otherwise, we're no longer living in the 1950s. Husbands must play a part in keeping the house orderly. That's OK, because you're a man: creative, adaptive, and able to overcome any obstacle. A little housekeeping needn't cut into valuable guy time.

- **Turn home repairs into a social activity.** What are friends for if not to come over and help you fix the leaky sink? For the price of a few beers, you can live up to your responsibilities *and* hang with the dudes.

- **Don't turn off that football game!** The game is a perfect time to vacuum, fold clothes, or do other autopilot tasks easily accomplished while keeping tabs on the score. And while you're at it . . .

- **Learn to love sports on the radio.** Its joys are many, but one is that you can easily stay abreast of the game while power-washing the deck or repainting the bedroom.

- **Don't let the dishes pile up.** That way, they never become overwhelming. Wash glasses and utensils as you use them to stave off imposing piles.

- **Yardwork is like playing.** Cue up some music, invite a few friends, fill the cooler, and watch in satisfaction as your busy Saturday afternoon turns into a productive good time.

- **Schedule non-chores, too.** Establish a regular weekday as pure, *official*, leisure-only guy time—and, in fairness, be sure your wife does the same for girl time. Insist on it. Chores should never intrude on this time for either of you.

Ten Commandments Regarding Laundry

You're sharing a house, you're sharing your lives, and you're sharing piles and piles of clothes. In the grand scheme of things, those clothing piles are the easy part, right? Think again. Few things are more personal than what we wear on our body, and that means the laundry is more than a chore—it's a science. It is also a test every husband must pass. But don't fret. Armed with these few simple rules, even a reformed single guy can survive the laundry minefield.

1. If your wife usually does the laundry, offer to do it.

2. Good laundry begins and ends with good sorting.

3. Always read the label. Different fabrics require different temperatures and drying strategies—and hell hath no fury like a woman whose dry-clean-only garments you just sent through the spin cycle.

4. Colors and whites do not mix.

5. Colors and bleach do not mix.

6. Don't overload the machine.

7. Consider using eco-friendly detergents.

8. If you put a cotton garment in the dryer for the first time, it *will* shrink a little. Consider hang-drying instead.

9. Do not hang-dry the wife's unmentionables anywhere visible if guests might be stopping by.

10. Bad folding is worse than no folding at all.

How to Fold Clothes

If you're anything like the author, your clothes-folding skills leave a lot to be desired. Folding the clothes is possibly second only to washing the dishes on the Most Hated Chores list, and that means only one thing: A good husband should know how to step in and carry his share of the burden. Your wife will love you for it. Here's how to fold clothes without looking like you just stepped out of a college dormitory.

1. If the clothes aren't fully dry, don't fold them. Unless, that is, you *like* to smell musty.

2. Sort the clean laundry by category: pants, shirts, items to be hung, undergarments, etc. (Note: Creased pants are for hanging.)

3. Hang dress shirts immediately. Once on the hanger, button as if being worn. This may make it harder to remove them, but it will also improve their look and life span. (Note: No wire hangers!)

4. Hold dress pants flat from the front and

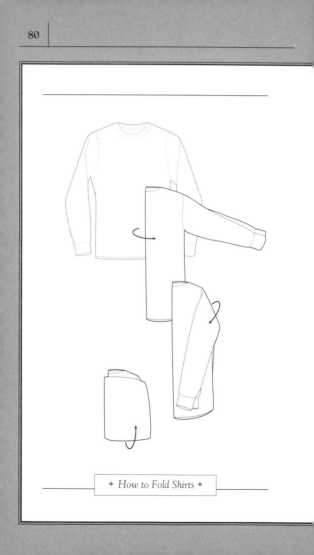

✦ *How to Fold Shirts* ✦

rear so they naturally fold at the crease. Drape over a hanger so they are halved roughly at the knee.

5. Lay dress socks together and fold in half (top to bottom). Stack. Lay tube socks together, grasp the opening of one sock, and neatly invert both socks through the opening.

6. Fold shirts vertically (right to left) so they look like half shirts. Fold the sleeves over the body of the shirt, then fold horizontally, with the sleeves inside the fold.

7. Fold pants legs together, pockets to the outside. Bring the bottom of the pant legs up until they meet the waistband.

8. Skirts can be folded like shirts, but are better hung. Defer to your wife.

Outdoor Maintenance Essentials

Fact: Outdoor maintenance stinks. Also a fact: You have to do it anyway. Third fact? You can skate by on some easy basics without becoming Yard-Obsessed Dude.

- **Tree branches:** Trees are wonderful, but they can also tear up your siding, drop seeds into your gutters that will grow into weeds, interfere with power lines, and block your or your neighbors' windows. Keep an eye on them and trim when necessary.

- **Sticks and stones:** All that junk in your yard, in addition to being a safety hazard, makes mowing, home improvement, and landscaping more difficult. Remove it twice a year. Use junk stones for a rain garden; send sticks and wood debris to your fire pit.

- **Gutters:** Gutters play a vital role in the tiny infrastructure system that is your house. Blockages can cause big problems, including leaks and flooding. Have them cleaned biannually.

- **Weeds:** A weed is any plant you don't want. Skip the chemicals whenever possible. Pull weeds up at the roots when possible. You'll have to weed a few times a year, but that's a small price to pay for healthy soil and cleaner drinking water.

Intro to Lawn Care

A man with a house is a man with a lawn, and a lawn is a man's pride and joy—maybe even more than his restored muscle car. When it comes time to maintain your pride and joy, keep these tips in mind.

- You don't need to water constantly. Let nature do its job. When you do water, let your lawn drink deeply.

- The best time to water is early morning, right around dawn.

- Mow weekly if possible, unless your lawn isn't growing. Frequent mowing helps grass develop healthy roots.

- Avoid mowing if the grass is wet.

- When mowing during hot weather, keep the mower blades at the highest (farthest from the ground) setting. That will prevent the sun from burning the most sensitive part of the blade.

- Mow in straight lines. On each pass, overlap the previous line slightly. Every few mowings, switch directions (i.e., go front to back instead of side to side, or vice versa).

- Worms are great for the soil. If you've already got 'em, great. If not, buy some at a bait shop and release them in your yard (preferably on a rainy night, so the birds don't get them before they can burrow into the ground).

How to Fix a Clogged Toilet or Sink

It's inevitable. The toilet is going to back up. The sink is going to overflow. A pipe will become clogged. And you will have to call upon your manly birthright as Fixer of Clogs to get the water flowing again.

Toilet:

1. Skip the chemicals. Even when they work they're slow, and if they don't you'll have a toilet full of toxic water on your hands.

2. Grab a plunger. Plungers with a suction-cup end are close to useless on toilets. Invest in one with a fat bell end.

3. Place the end of the plunger into the toilet bowl, completely covering the hole in the bottom. Thrust once, slowly and gently to create suction, and then release quickly.

4. If the first thrust did not clear the blockage, repeat several times in rapid but measured succession, about two seconds apart.

5. Still clogged? You need a plumbing snake, aka an auger (cost: $5 to $15). Wearing rubber gloves, feed the snake into the toilet until you feel the obstruction. Twist it in a clockwise direction. Push and twist until the snake pushes through. The obstruction will give way, or you can draw it out with the snake.

Sink:

1. If your pipes are made of metal, use boiling water first. Slowly pour a full pot of boiling water directly into the drain. If it does not dissolve the blockage, or if you have PVC pipes instead of metal pipes, move to step 2.

2. Try a plunger, as above—but don't use the same plunger! (Ewwww.) On sinks, suction-cup plungers are best.

3. No luck? Try a pass with the snake.

4. Still not cleared? Now the work begins. Place a bucket or pan beneath the sink. You're going to be opening a pipe and will need to catch any water still inside.

5. That little S-curve in the pipe is called the "trap." You're going to remove it. Traps differ from home to home; yours may not match what is described here. But, as we've discussed before, you're a man, and you'll adapt.

6. Using a pipe wrench, loosen and remove the slip nuts at each end of the trap. Empty the water into the pan. Some traps will instead have a pull-out plug at the bottom; if yours does, remove it.

7. Using the snake, push slowly inward, moving in a circular motion to get past the curves in the pipe. When you feel an obstruction, gently screw into it with the snake, using clockwise twists. Continue until you feel you've moved past the obstruction and then attempt to draw it out.

8. Reattach the piping and flush with hot (but *not* boiling) water.

How to Hire a Handyman

You're a man's man. Screwdrivers and hammers bend to your every command. Nails tremble in your presence. Home repairs are your lifeblood. Or, you know, maybe not. In either case, sometimes even you need to throw in the towel and hire a professional.

1. Have a clear idea of your needs before making the first call. Write them down.

2. Depending on the work you need done, a jack-of-all-trades handyman might suffice. However, detailed electrical or plumbing repairs will probably require a specialist.

3. Before hitting the yellow pages, ask friends and coworkers if they can recommend someone. Getting referrals is better than hiring from a random advertisement.

4. We know you want to get the work done fast, but don't hire the first person you speak to; line up several prospects.

5. Does your contractor have liability insurance? If not, keep looking.

6. If you're hiring a specialist, inquire whether he or she is licensed with your state. If not, keep looking.

7. Request references, and be sure to check them.

8. Check with the Better Business Bureau, state licensing agencies, or local consumer protection organizations to see if complaints have been lodged against the contractor.

9. Ask for an estimate, and *get it in writing*. Clarify if you will be billed by the hour or at a flat rate. If you agree to hire the contractor, put your maximum budget in writing as well. Unscrupulous contractors may slam you with additional costs if an agreement is not in writing.

Meet Your Circuit Breaker

The circuit breaker is the single most important piece of equipment in your home. It controls the flow of electricity, cutting power if there is too much and preventing all that wonderful energy from burning the place to the ground. Here is what you need to know.

- A circuit breaker is essentially a board of switches located behind a small steel door and set into the wall.

- It's probably in a basement or utility closet, though the location varies from house to house.

- Each switch controls power to a small number of outlets/switches in the house. They should be, but sometimes aren't, clearly labeled.

- If more power is being sucked down by one portion of the house than the electrical system can bear, it will trip the circuit, which is another way of saying that it cuts off the flow of power.

- Resetting the power is easy. Turn off lights and unplug appliances/electronic devices in the affected section of the house. Open the circuit box. Flip the appropriate switch. Power should return.

- If the breaker keeps tripping whenever you use a certain electrical device, that device is causing a problem. Find somewhere else to plug it in.

Note: Older homes may have a fuse box instead of a circuit breaker. They serve the same function, but fuses are slightly more of a nuisance to reset: Instead of flippable switches, they're little plugs that burn out and need to be replaced. The good news is they're just a few dollars at any hardware store, and all you have to do is pull out the blown one and plug in the new one.

How to Make the Bed

When you're single, the bed only gets made when your parents are visiting or you're bringing a girl home— and maybe not even then. Marriage, however, is another ballgame. There will be plenty of chaos in your life; your bed should be a peaceful and relaxing sanctuary every day.

1. Once or twice a week, pull off the pillows, blankets, and linens (flat and fitted sheets).

2. Put a fresh fitted sheet over the mattress, pulling the elastic corners around the corners at the head of the bed first. Pull tightly from the foot of the bed, securing the remaining two corners there.

3. Smooth the fitted sheet from the middle, then tuck the nonelastic sides under the mattress.

4. Spread a clean flat sheet over the bed, with the wide hem at the head of the bed, roughly where the pillows will be. Smooth out the sheet.

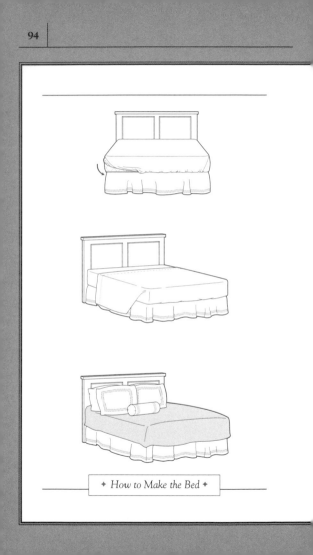

• How to Make the Bed •

5. Lift the foot of the mattress and tuck the sheet beneath it. Follow with the sides, starting from the foot of the bed and working to the head.

6. Lay a blanket or comforter overtop, starting at the head and spreading it evenly from the center. The blanket should not be pink, nor should it have pretty birds and flowers on it.

7. Cover the pillows in new pillowcases if necessary, and then arrange them at the head of the bed.

8. Call your wife into the room and think of an excuse to unmake the bed.

Your Stuff: Use It, Store It, Throw It Away

The author would like to make a confession: He is a hoarder. And, boy, is that a bad habit, because learning how to manage the amazing amount of stuff we husbands can accumulate is something we all need to do.

- **Use it.** If the "stuff" is something you use regularly, keep it easily accessible. Open shelves are great for accessible storage. If you don't have the luxury of space, consider affordable organizers from office supply or home goods stores. Even better, for a great Man Project, build your own.

- **Store it.** Storage is easy. Simple solutions include egg crates and banker's boxes, stackable cardboard boxes available at any office supply store. Clearly label all boxes. Store only those things you know you won't be using in the next six months but that you will need within the next two years. Otherwise . . .

- **Get rid of it.** Unless you have a specific and attainable plan for it, any object you haven't looked at in two years needs to be at the bottom of a recycling bin, on a table at a yard sale, donated to a local charity, or thrown away. A small handful of sentimental items get a pass—keywords being *small handful*. Lose the rest.

How to Rid the Home of a Spider

Spider-wrangling is a husband's sworn duty. Your instinct may be to squash it and get back to the game, but hold that shoe. Bugs are bad. Spiders eat bugs. So why not let the spider work do your dirty work by capturing it and moving it to your outer perimeter?

1. Identify the spider. Most are harmless, but you don't want to mess with black widows and brown recluses. The recluse is brown, small to medium in size, and marked with a violin-shape pattern on its head. The widow is shiny black, with an hourglass mark on its abdomen. If you are bit by either, seek medical attention right away.

2. If the spider is on a flat surface, such as a wall or ceiling, great. This will be easy. Grab a clear container with a lid and position yourself just under arm's length from your enemy.

3. If the spider is not on a flat surface, you'll

have to coax it to one. Using a long, straight object (ruler, broom handle, spatula), poke near the spider. It will skitter away. Guide its movement to an open area. Be careful not to smash it!

4. Hold the open mouth of the container at a forearm's length from your prey, then quickly cap it on top of the beast.

5. Gently slide the container so that the edge nudges the spider trapped beneath it. The goal is for the spider to cling to the inside of the container.

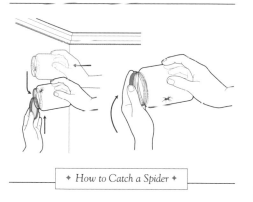

✦ How to Catch a Spider ✦

6. Once the spider is clinging to the inside, slide the lid between the wall and its cage. Trapped!

7. Dump your new friend somewhere outside. Congratulations: You've put one critter out, and it will eat others that might otherwise get in.

Five Important Vehicle Maintenance Protocols

You don't need to be an automobile expert to keep these essentials in mind—and, just as important, to impart them to your wife.

- **Check the oil.** Locate the release lever for the hood, which is usually located to the left of the steering wheel. After popping the hood, look for the colored handle marked "oil." Pull it out, wipe the stick clean with a rag, reinsert it, and pull it out again. If the oil line doesn't fall between the two marks at the end, you need to add a quart. If the oil on the stick is black, time to get it changed.

- **Check the tires.** The tires on most passenger vehicles have an ideal tire pressure of 32 to 35 PSI when cold (i.e., when you haven't been driving). Unscrew the cap from the doodad sticking out of your tire and pop a tire pressure gauge on it. If the pressure is too high, your car will handle poorly; too low, and your tires will wear quickly. Correct tire pressure also improves gas mileage.

- **Wiper blades.** Blinded by rain even when the wipers are on? Check the blades for wear. Replacement is easy.

- **Spare tire.** Be sure your car has a usable spare, either a "donut" (a plastic wheel good for limited, slow travel) or a full spare. Periodically verify that full spares have ample air.

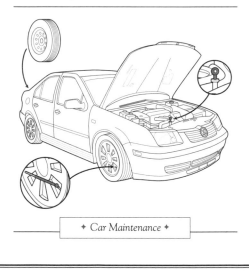

✦ Car Maintenance ✦

- **Regular tune-ups.** Essential to a long car life. Check your car manual for the optimal tune-up schedule, and stick to it. Don't have a manual? Then bring your car in every two years or 30,000 miles, whichever comes first.

The Joy of Tax Returns

The days when a layperson could understand income taxes are long gone. Oh, and you're married? Welcome to seven more layers of complexity.

- **See an expert.** No shame here. An expert will help you get every dollar owed to you. National chains are fine, but local experts with a personal stake in your business are better.

- **Deductions.** If you had to spend money to make money or get a job, you can deduct it. Some healthcare and house-related costs can be deducted, too.

- **Withholdings.** Having Uncle Sam withhold a lot gives you a smaller paycheck but larger tax returns. Think of it as a forced savings account. If you don't want Uncle Sam earning interest on your money, keep your withholdings small. But be prepared to write the government a check each April.

- **Joint or separate returns?** The only good reason to file separately is if you're trying

to hide income from your spouse of if
you're separated at the time of filing. Many
tax credits are available only if you file
joint tax returns.

- **Key paperwork to save.** Pay stubs,
especially for independent work. Health
insurance/HMO payments. Property tax
records. Bank statements. IRA, mutual
fund, annuity, and other investment statements. Scholarships. Education expenses,
student loans, and bank loans. Records of
charitable giving.

Ten Things Every Married Man Should Have

Man is beast: a machine made to hunt and eat and reproduce. Put tools in his hands, however, and he becomes a creature capable of building entire civilizations . . . with a little help from his wife, of course. If building and maintaining a marriage is akin to building and maintaining a civilization—and it is—these are the tools essential for every married man's lifelong quest to civilize the beast within.

1. A small toolbox with the essentials for basic home improvements: hammer, screwdrivers, measuring tape, pliers, etc.

2. Two pairs of dress shoes (brown and black).

3. A family AAA membership.

4. Duct tape. There is nothing it can't do.

5. A nice suit. Classic, not trendy.

6. A semi-expensive leisure item that must be used away from home (e.g., golf clubs, a mountain bike, skis).

7. A couch comfortable enough to sleep on.

8. A legal will and life insurance policy.

9. Health insurance. When you're single you can let this slide. But you're not single anymore.

10. At least one photo of your wife (and kids) on your person at all times.

Regarding the

FAMILY

Four Lousy Reasons to Have a Child (and Three Good Ones)

The decision to have a child is the biggest a person can make. If you're going to create a tiny person who will rely on you and learn from you, it's best to do it for the right reasons . . . because there are *plenty* of lousy reasons.

Lousy Reasons:

1. *"All our friends are having them."* We've all been there. But keeping up with the Joneses is a reason for planting flowers in your yard, not for creating a new human life.

2. *"Our relationship is on the rocks; this will bring us closer together."* No, it won't. It will exacerbate the problems in your relationship, not to mention ruin your child's youth.

3. *"Who will take care of us when we're old?"* Take care of you? More like leave you as soon as possible. Begin a family on such a selfish note and be prepared for children who resent the life you gave them.

4. *"My/Her parents are pressuring us to."* Let's just cut to the chase: It's not their call. Allow others to guide a decision of this magnitude and you may as well turn over the keys to your marriage.

Good Reasons:

1. *To create a family.* For many, the idea of marriage is inextricably interwoven with the idea of starting a family. If this seems obvious to you, that might be a good sign that it's reason enough.

2. *To share your love with another.* You and your wife are binary stars pumping out so much light a single solar system cannot contain you. How better to use that love than to direct some of it toward a little tiny you?

3. *It feels right.* Yes, it's based purely on emotion, and, yes, you should make sure you're both prepared for it first. But if you both feel strongly that a child is the next logical step in your relationship, that's just Mother Nature telling you that you're ready.

How to Live with a Pregnant Wife

Marriage is hard. Parenthood is hard. Pregnancy? *Really* hard, even if you're the man. There is no strapping on your boots and solving the problem; there is only learning to cope. Here are a few things to keep in mind:

- **Don't compare your frustration to hers.** Just don't. Sure, this pregnancy is throwing your comfortable life for a loop. But how do you think the lady with the basketball in her uterus feels?

- **Ease off on the vices.** Smoking, drinking, skydiving—whatever your usual poison, your job for these nine months is to suffer alongside your wife, who's temporarily forbidden from doing these things. Show some solidarity.

- **Sex is not off limits (unless she says it is).** Your wife is not a delicate flower. Sex during pregnancy is perfectly safe for both your wife and your baby. More important, she may be in need of love and affection.

Make her feel wanted during this emotional time.

- **Indulge her food cravings (as long as they're not medically problematic).** Cravings are real. Indulge them. Yes, that means dashing to the store at midnight for Marshmallow Fluff and Genoa salami. Don't complain. Just suck it up and get it done.

- **Sleeping won't be easy.** Not for you and certainly not for her. Be patient, and give up as much of the bed as she needs. She'll need it.

What Happens in the Delivery Room

If you break out in a cold sweat thinking about being in the delivery room during childbirth, you're not alone. Sure, Mom has it pretty tough in there, what with all the pain and the pushing and the pain. Did we mention the pain? But Dad also needs to be prepared for the uglier side of this miracle, because the days of being sequestered in the waiting room are over. We've all seen scream-filled birth scenes on TV, but what should you *really* expect in the delivery room?

- **Expect mixed feelings.** You're going to experience something wonderful, but you're also going to see your wife—and her body—in ways you never have before.

- **If you can't watch the actual birth, don't be ashamed.** Many men can't. Stand by your wife's side, hold her hand, give her your love and support, and don't feel obligated to watch things you don't want to watch.

- **One more time: Your wife will be in pain.** Pain like you've never seen. Nonetheless, your role is limited. Offer your hand or arm for mangling as she deals with the pain. Give her ice chips when she asks. Beyond that, you're useless.

- **The pushing is neither quick nor easy.** It's not like on television. This can go on for hours. Practice patience.

- **There will be blood.** Birthing is a messy business.

- **Bowel movements happen.** You read that right: Your wife just might have a bowel movement while in labor. She'll probably be self-conscious about it. No matter how gross you think it is, Do. *Not*. Comment. On it.

- **Caesarean section?** There is no gentle way to put this: You might see her internal organs. If you have a weak stomach, make sure the area is screened when the cutting begins.

- **Be prepared for an ugly alien.** When Mini-You is born, Mini-You will not be a neat and clean and cuddly baby. Newborns are usually covered in goo. Often they're a strange color: blue or mauve or apricot, for instance. Oh—and the major case of conehead. This is normal.

- **You might cry.** It's OK. Men cry, sometimes about things other than the World Series. This is as good a time as any.

How to Make Family Time (Even If You Work a Lot)

Before you start a family, days contain 24 hours. Once children are a part of your life, Einstein's Special Theory of Relativity dictates that days will suddenly, unaccountably, seem to last only 15 hours. Between working, sleeping, chores, and errands, it can be hard to find time just to enjoy your family's company. Here's how to triumph over the nefarious clock.

- **Consolidate your trips.** Running errands are a weekend ritual in the author's household. Doing them all in one trip—banking, shopping, etc.—saves a bundle of time. It also plays directly into the next tip.

- **Turn errands into family outings.** Need to drop by the home goods center for a tool? Bring the family. Let the kids get a little something. Maybe some wood. (Kids love wood.) Getting car repairs? Take the family, and go have a few slices of pizza while you wait. Use road games and conversation to make errands fun.

- **Get the kids involved.** Tackling a major home project? Have them "help." Even if their help involves standing around peppering you with questions, you'll be building relationships with them.

- **Don't fill every weekend.** Yes, weekends are when you catch up on work around the house or squeeze in some increasingly rare socializing, but be sure to keep time open for just you and the family. Even if you have to turn down social engagements.

- **Adjust your meal times.** Depending on your work schedule, you may want to place extra emphasis on breakfast, using that as a time for the family to dine together. Or, if you work late, consider having a later dinner. Studies repeatedly show that families who eat together are happier and healthier.

How Not to Fight over Money

Seeing as so many of life's problems center on dollars and cents, it's no wonder that money is so often at the root of marital problems. Here are five things to keep in mind when it comes to the green.

- **First rule of breadwinner's club: Don't talk about breadwinner's club.** If you are the primary earner, don't lord it over your spouse. If she is, don't make it an issue. You're in this together.

- **Make a budget.** Know your income, calculate your expenses, and create a budget. And, mostly important, stick to it.

- **Give yourself some breathing room.** A tight budget often leads to tension, and tension means fights. Your budget should include enough breathing room for emergencies, treating yourself when needed, and saving whenever possible.

- **Agree on basic rules.** Maybe no purchases over $500 without consulting each other, or reasonable personal allowances, or income from a certain source always goes toward a certain bill. Guidelines such as these will put you both on the same page, which will in turn help you to avoid fights.

- **Spend together; save together.** You don't get to splurge while she stays frugal. You shouldn't have an empty wallet while she fills the closet with shoes. Feast or famine, make sure you're always in the same boat.

How to Change a Diaper

Not inclined to reenact scenes from bad Hollywood comedies? Want to give the Missus a well-deserved break? With a little practice and patience, you can change diapers like a champion.

1. You'll need to have on hand a clean diaper, wipes, lotion or cream (if necessary), and a small plastic trash bag.

2. Place a towel on the changing surface and lay your baby on her back. Unfasten the diaper tabs.

3. Lift the baby's bottom by gently holding onto her ankles. Just a few inches will do. Slide the dirty diaper out from underneath her, using the clean portions of the diaper to scoop up excess poop.

4. Clean her bottom and genitals with baby wipes. Clean from front to back, not back to front. This will prevent infections, especially with girls. If your baby is a newborn,

avoid wipes that contain alcohol, which can cause rashes.

5. Slide the clean diaper under your baby's bottom. The diaper should be marked so that you place the tabs facing the right way.

6. If you have doctor-recommended ointments or creams, apply them now.

7. Pull the front of the diaper between her legs and over her stomach. Fasten. Be sure the diaper is snug enough to prevent leaks, but not so snug as to cause discomfort.

8. Dispose of soiled diaper and wipes in the trash bag. Wash your hands thoroughly. Fecal matter can cause disease.

How to Side with Your Wife, Not Your Mother

One of the most difficult things a married man can face is a clash between his wife and his mother. Your instinct may be to steer clear—twice the fury for your troubles, after all—but you're a big boy now, and a married one at that. You are committed to supporting your wife. But how to walk this tightrope without plunging to disaster? It's tricky, but it can be done.

- **Have a heart-to-heart with your wife.** If she knows you're there for her and support her, it will be that much easier to help ease her anger. And don't just tell her—*show* her through your actions.

- **Never allow your mother to bad-mouth your wife.** Be respectful but firm when you tell her that you will not tolerate it. Then remind your mother that you love her. The message you send will be powerful.

- **Stand together.** If you disagree with your wife, do so privately.

- **Don't force the issue.** You can't make them like each other. With time they'll either grow to respect each other or learn to stay out of the other's way.

- **Don't let your wife cut you off from your mother.** Let her know you stand behind her, but that a fractured family is unacceptable. Your wife can keep her distance in the interest of peace, but that shouldn't apply to you, too.

- **Never let kids become pawns in a dispute.** This rule is unbreakable.

She Loves the Kids More Than She Loves You

This title may sound harsh to you. A little too direct. Maybe a bit uncomfortable. But it's an important fact, and one that you have to know.

Your wife is the love of your life. And you have been hers. But when children enter the picture, you cease to be Love No. 1.

And that's perfectly fine. Natural. Expected. Not something to worry about.

Think of your own mother. Even if you had the healthiest white-picket-fence upbringing imaginable, you were probably still a massive pain in her tush at times, and she probably returned the favor by being one in yours. Despite that, she loves you as unconditionally as it's possible to love someone. After all, she carried you around *inside her body*. Wiped the poo from your butt. Endured being assaulted by your *urine and vomit*. And still she loves you.

When you and your wife have children, her offspring become the most important thing in her life. It is her biological imperative. It's not a feeling she could avoid even if she wanted to. It's as hard-wired in her as scratching your butt is in you. But the fact that she loves the kids more than you doesn't mean she doesn't love you. Quite the opposite. You are the father of her children; her love for you, even if under the surface, is now at an all-time high. You are bonded for life; she can never forget that. Yeah, she loves the kids more . . . but she's *supposed* to. It's the way Nature wants things to be.

So relax and be proud of it. You picked a good wife, and now she's a good mother.

Husband Tips for Hosting a Family Gathering

Ahhh, the large family gathering. Even with the best relatives in the world, hosting can be a handful. With all that food to manage, personalities to massage, and messes to deal with, you might be inclined to lock yourself away until it's over. No need for extreme measures, though; there's no reason why this can't be easy.

- **Music is essential.** Music fills gaps in conversation, gives people something to talk about, and just plain makes everyone feel good. Don't rely on the radio, though—commercials are not relaxing. Mix your own music.

- **Give the kids chores.** Pretend work is a "special mission," and suddenly it's easy to get kids to play along. Instruct them to snatch up empty plates, cups, and bottles. It's their secret assignment. They'll keep at it all day, and cleanup later will be that much easier.

- **Food: Keep it simple, stupid.** Food is an essential ingredient to a family gathering. But unless you've got a real chef on board, don't get crazy ambitious. The less complexity, the fewer things you'll have to juggle and the more likely you are to avoid complaints from finicky Aunt Joyce.

- **Save the spousal arguments for later.** Family gatherings are NOT the time to air your differences. *No matter what.*

- **Have a fail-safe.** If contentious family conversation arises, have a distraction ready to go. A few decks of cards, the latest photos of the kids, Jell-O Twister— anything to pull the grumps away from their grumpiness.

- **Invite a friend.** Having a close friend on hand can be all it takes to keep you mellow in the midst of family insanity, so don't be afraid to call for backup.

Managing Your Erotic Materials

Keeping your various knickknacks and collectibles out on a shelf is great, but some of your literature and movies might be a bit, well, delicate for such public displays. Whether you and the wife partake together or it's your own private stash, knowing how to manage your erotic materials is essential.

Your Private Stash

- *Deep folders, marked discs.* Chances are, your happy fun-time material will be on the computer. Store it in deeply hidden folders with specific but obscure faux-technical names like "Drive Boot Data" or on discs labeled obsoletely (e.g., "Windows 3.1 Backup").

- *Just the essentials.* Keep only what you'll return to. Do you really want your wife to stumble across 58 gigs of happy fun pictures?

- *Have a "porn buddy."* Ever hear that phrase, "A friend helps you move; a real friend helps you move a body?" Well, add to the end: "or your porn." Your trusted pal's task? To get rid of your stash should anything unexpectedly tragic happen to you.

The Marital Stash

- *Her closet, not yours.* Let her control the stuff.

- *Your labels, please.* Whether on discs, thumb drives, or in boxes, mark your materials with code uninteresting to kids ("Car repair manuals") and that won't attract the attention of snooping guests.

- *No Internet connection.* If your happy fun time stash involves homemade materials, never, *ever* store it on a computer with an Internet connection. A compromised system = your private moments on a dozen unsavory sites.

Rules for Borrowing Money from Your Parents

The dreaded day may come when you have to (gulp!) go to your (or her) parents to borrow money. Don't be ashamed; this is part of what it means to be family. But before you do, set yourself some ground rules.

1. **Forget your discomfort.** This is family. It's why we cherish the idea of family in the first place.

2. **Your reasons better be good.** In emergency debt or need a boost to add the new baby room? Great. Want to upgrade your TV or just need some cash? Not so great. This is a matter of trust. Make it count.

3. **Have a payback plan.** Before you even ask, know how and when you'll repay the loan. No need to worry about setting a rigid payment structure; just have a handle on how you can realistically return the money.

4. **Treat gifts like loans.** Even if they say it's a gift, plan on paying them back. If not in cash, then in some other way: treating them to a vacation, doing work at their house, or other similar offer.

5. **Loans aren't a weapon.** If you get the sense it will be held over your head, consider another option. The signs are there that this might be a family-splitter.

Alone with the Kids, Part I: What Not to Do

It's just you and the kids—and that is a frightening prospect, indeed. It's not that you're not a good father; it's that without your wife around, the kids turn into frantic balls of insanity and you go from a controlled, capable man to a helpless wreck. Fret not: All will be well.

- **Turn off the football game—and keep it off.** You might say you're sharing your love of the sport, but the only person you're fooling is yourself.

- **Stay awake!** You can't supervise the kids if you're asleep.

- **Save movies and video games until they're older.** Sure, these diversions might keep young kids occupied in the short term, but you'll regret it later when their attention spans are shorter than this book.

- **Alcohol.** If it's just you and the kids, put down the bottle. You can't be responsible and react to emergencies if you're half in the bag.

- **Don't speak ill of your wife, not even in jest.** Children take humor differently than adults do, and the message you send won't do them any favors in their own relationships. Worst of all: They'll tell on you.

- **No fireworks.** Trust us on this.

Alone with the Kids, Part II: What to Do

Don't let the dire warnings of the last entry scare you. Not only does time alone with the kids not have to be intimidating, it can be the kind of fun you never realized you were missing. Sprinkle some of these suggestions into your babysitting schedule and soon you'll be begging for more alone time with the kids.

- **Finger painting.** Every kid loves it, and if you do things right—put plenty of newspaper down on the table!—you'll love it, too. Hang the results on the fridge for Mom to see, or make them gifts for the grandparents.

- **Show them how to play a board game.** Something simple like Sorry! or Chutes and Ladders is perfect for younger children. We bet you've forgotten how fun those games can be.

- **Make up a crazy story together.** Set the scene ("It was a dark and stormy night . . ."), let the kids add a little, you add a little, and just keep going until you're all dying from laughter.

- **Go explore the world.** If there is a park or a patch of woods, go walking in it. Pretend it's an adventure.

- **Introduce them to music.** Play a few of your favorites and encourage the kids to sing or dance along. An early love for music is a gift they'll cherish forever.

- **Play catch.** This never gets old. Ever.

Vacations to Make Everyone Happy

It might be easier to bring peace to the Middle East than it is to plan a vacation that will please everyone. But like any good international coalition—just go with us on this analogy, OK?—it's part of what you signed up for when you said "I do." Here's how to ensure your family vacations put a smile on every family member's face.

- **Don't pack the schedule.** No matter where you go, leave breathing room in your plans. Doing so will allow you to adjust plans as needed. (Example: Mammoth Cave National Park, Kentucky. Exciting and safe spelunking, with lots of downtime.)

- **Keep dinner plans simple.** If your days are filled with go, go, go, make your dinner slow, slow, slow. You'll appreciate winding down after a hectic day. Tip: Let whoever wasn't the day's focus choose where to eat. (Example: Any pizza joint in the northeast. Quick, easy, low-key, and delicious.)

- **Front-load kids' stuff.** Even patient kids want their fun now. If your family vacation includes good times and theme parks, do these near the start and save the boring adult stuff for later. Kids will be so drained from thrill rides that you'll get a few days of peace. (Example: Disney's Magic Kingdom, Florida or California. Can't go wrong with a classic, especially one that's fun for both kids and adults.)

- **Plan a low-key final day.** Want to go back to work just as stressed as when you left? Then run yourself ragged until the minute it's time to go home. If not, then plan a final day of quiet relaxation. (Example: Yellowstone National Park, Wyoming. The excitement of breathtaking natural wonders won't wear you down.)

- **Education can be fun.** Vacations don't need to be thrill rides and crowded beaches. A trip to a historic community can offer good times you may not have imagined, with something for Dad, Mom, and the kids. (Example: Colonial Williamsburg, Virginia. A pint in a

Revolution era tavern? Shopping for classic dresses and knickknacks? Watching
George Washington's soldiers drill in full
uniform? Check, check, and check.)

- **Research the surrounding area.** Wherever
your chosen vacation, scope out a nearby
day trip that differs from the main event:
zoos, minor-league baseball teams, mini-
golf courses, museums. (Example: Six
Flags, anywhere. Most Six Flags amuse-
ment parks draw other attractions, from
horseback riding to golf and more.)

How to Say "I Love You" (Let's Count the Ways!)

- Casually, on your way out the door in the morning
- After a long, passionate kiss
- With a note left in her purse
- In French: *Je t'aime* or *je t'adore*
- With a random phone call in the middle of the day
- With her favorite flowers
- In front of your friends
- In Italian: *Ti amo*
- After dinner (*every* dinner)
- Randomly popping your head in the shower (while sneaking a peek)
- After she gives birth to your child
- In front of her parents
- In Japanese: *Anata ga daisuki desu*
- With passion, whenever she's done something nice for you

- After making love
- In a letter mailed to her for no reason at all
- In J. R. R. Tolkien's Elvish: *Amin mela lle*
- With a song
- In front of your children
- On any day ending in the letter "y"

Stuff You Should Know but I Can't Tell You

- Your Social Security number
- Your wife's birthday
- Your anniversary
- The location of important household documents
- The phone number for your doctor's office
- Your family's medical history
- Your wife's family's medical history
- Your wife's friend's ex-husband's sister's name (because she'll expect you to know it)
- When and how you met your wife
- Where you first kissed
- What turns your wife on
- What gifts she likes to receive
- Where her G-spot is
- Her current bra, dress, and shoe sizes

Stuff I Should Say after Writing This Book

Major thanks to Stephen Segal, for being a great editor and a great guy, and to everyone at Quirk Books; thanks for having me on board.

I would also be remiss if I didn't thank the slew of folks at my Internet haunts for their tireless support and excellent suggestions. You know who you are, and you know why you rock.

Most of all, my thanks—and my heart—go out to Natalie. You make me a better person. This book is for you . . . even all the parts I don't actually live up to.